··PHYSICS··

··ASTRONOMY··

··SCIENCES··

NEW THEORIES

WITH

INTERPRETATIONS

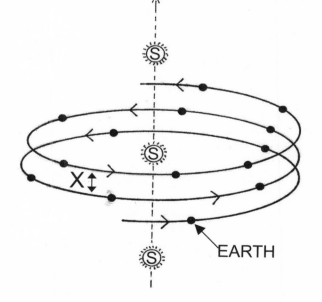

EARTH

Walter H. Volkmann

Every effort has been made to avoid errors, but despite best efforts, some will appear. Please bring these errors to my attention, so they can be corrected in future editions.

First Printing 2005 4000 copies

Volkmann, Walter H.

Physics – Astronomy – Sciences
New Theories with Interpretations

Includes Index

ISBN 0-9765228-0-2

Cover: Illustration see page 104

Printed in the United States of America
by Taylor Publishing Co. Dallas, Texas

Table of Contents

Chapter   **Page**

INTRODUCTION TO THE BOOK

This book is for thinkers, those who have an inquisitive mind. Think each sentence as you read, many times one sentence will have lot of information. The book will not have a lot of superfluous writing or information.

In this book, you will find mostly new theories that are not to be found in the textbooks, and as far as I know, are not to be found anywhere. It may be difficult to understand and accept the new theories because they are new and unfamiliar.

Chapter 8, "Contraction of Length and Shrinkage of a "Mass With Energy," is confusing and difficult. You may have to read it more than once to get the meaning.

This book is written in a progressive manor. It is best to start at the beginning. Do not give up, as there is some very interesting information in later chapters.

I want to make the information accessible to a broad audience. Some science knowledge will help in understanding the information. High school science, first year college or first year university science is all the science one needs.

I have included many line drawings for better understanding of the written word. There are no hyphenated words at the end of a line to interrupt one's thoughts with trying to decide, "what is that word?"

Everything in the universe started with FORMATION ENERGY. You will read about FORMATION ENERGY in chapter 20.

Some of the new theories are "The Volkmann Effect, Movement of a MWE, with it's Self-Induced Back-Flux Resistance "The Volkmann Theory on Planet Formation," a new theory on dinosaur extinction and other theories.

This book has been a very laborious undertaking. A 100 times more than I thought at the start. It took almost all my extra hours. I was always short of hours to write and rewrite.

Many nights I would get up at 1:30 a.m. to study, going back to bed at 3:30 a. m. Everything was quiet, my mind was at it's best. Ideas seem to develop, racing through my mind as I was reading. Many good ideas were lost, due to the fact could not write them on paper fast enough. Before one thought was written, others were going through my mind.

It was an experience that happened many times. After the ideas were developed, I could hardly believe that this happened. The events that occurred were mysterious. I cannot fully explain.

Flower Mound, Texas   W. H. V.
December 2004

Acknowledgements
To

Jay Love – Taylor Publishing Company – Dallas, Texas
Thom Cashman – Wright Type Company – Dallas, Texas
Johnny Gomez – Graphics by Gomez – Dallas, Texas
Scott Young – Scott Young Photography – Flower Mound,
    Texas

Many thanks to the above named persons who helped with their professional knowledge & expertise to produce this book.

Mr. Love explained the book publishing process and sent me to Mr. Cashman to transform my hand-printed notes into a form that could be used to publish a book.

Mr. Cashman is a person with a lot of knowledge on preparing an author's work into a manuscript for the publisher to print a book. This requires a lot of patience trying to please the author and the publisher – a talent that he has.

Mr. Gomez is a professional graphic artist, who took my sketches and made them into the fine drawings you see in the book.

Mr. Young came to my home to take pictures of me in my study, so you the reader, could see the author and where he wrote the book.

And last of all, my wife Jeanette for her patience and help with typing certain parts of the book.

ABBREVIATIONS USED IN THIS WORK

AAU   As A Unit (Pulse Length)

EMS   Electromagnetic Spectrum

EMSE   Electromagnetic Spectrum Energy

EMSP   Electromagnetic Spectrum Pulses

EWM   Energy With Mass

EWOM   Energy Without Mass

FE   Formation Energy

GDO   Grid Dip Oscillator

GSMCE Galactic Space Medium Centrifugal Energy

GSME   Galactic Space Medium Energy

MWE   Mass With Energy

MWOE   Mass Without Energy

About the author

BIOGRAPHY

Walter H. Volkmann
Scientist

I have been in many fields of science since my early school years. In high school, I excelled in chemistry and physics. When I graduated from high school, my physics teacher tried to get me a scholarship, but due to the war, nothing could be done at the time.

My first job was at a testing laboratory, which tested cottonseed and its products. My second job was at a flour mill as a quality control chemist.

Then I had the opportunity to go to college in San Francisco, California. While going to college, I worked at a laboratory doing tests on alfalfa. Here I tested for carotene, using chromatography columns.

After college, I came back to Dallas, Texas. Being interested in radio, I studied for my amateur radio license, passed the test and received my license with the call letters W50MJ. I then studied for a commercial radio license and passed the test. With the extra knowledge of the commercial radio license, I was qualified to work on aircraft electronic equipment. I got a job with one of the large airlines.

Then I had the opportunity to go to work at a blood research center and as a chemist in the special chemistry laboratory at the associated hospital.

I was called into the Army, and was sent to their school for special training to help run one of their medical laboratories.

Afterwards I decided to go into business with my brother in the plant growing business. This business specialized in Saint Paulia (African Violets). At the time, growing plants by the tissue culture method was starting. To learn this method, I went to school for training at the Jones Cell Science Center at Lake Placid, New York. I went on to study at Pennsylvania State University to learn "Plant Biotechnology Methods", and following that, I went to the Center for Advanced Training in Cell and Molecular Biology.

I set up a plant tissue laboratory to grow plants by the tissue culture method. Before this, plant tissue culture training, I took a course called "McGraw-Hill Contemporary Electronics.

Now, here I am 80 years old, and writing this book!!

Walter H. Volkmann

Walter H. Volkmann

CHAPTER 1

MWE IS "MASS WITH ENERGY"
EWM IS "ENERGY WITH MASS"

What is now called MASS, will be referred to as Mass With Energy. It is the elements of the periodic table. There is no such thing as "Mass" by itself, it is MWE.

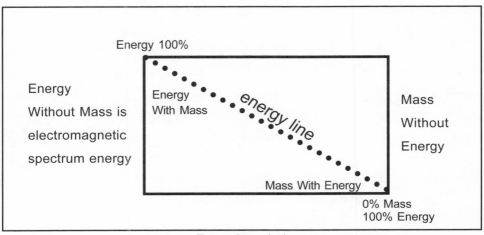

Drawing 1-1

Mass without energy does not exist. All Mass With Energy has been converted to Energy Without Mass.

New Theories with Interpretations

On the left side of the drawing 1-1 is the electromagnetic spectrum, just energy, no mass. All Mass With Energy has been converted to energy.

Mass Without Energy on the right of drawing 1-1 does not exist. Here all Mass With Energy has been converted to energy.

On the left side of the drawing 1-1 energy line, the dotted line going from 0% mass to 100% energy, is Energy Without Mass.

Supernovas, stars, sun and objects that give out electromagnetic energy are in the process of converting to Mass With Energy. In this process the energy is given out to receivers of this energy, being Mass With Energy. However, the process could go to all energy and no mass, if all the M in Mass With Energy is converted to electromagnetic spectrum energy. You will read more about this in Chapter 20, FORMATION ENERGY.

On the right side of the drawing 1-1 energy line Mass With Energy, I would put the periodic table of elements. The heavy elements are higher on the energy line than hydrogen. The heavy elements, that is the ones that have the most neutrons and other particles, as they would have more stored energy per atom.

CHAPTER 2

IN THE "MASS WITH ENERGY"
ATOM AND THE ELECTRON

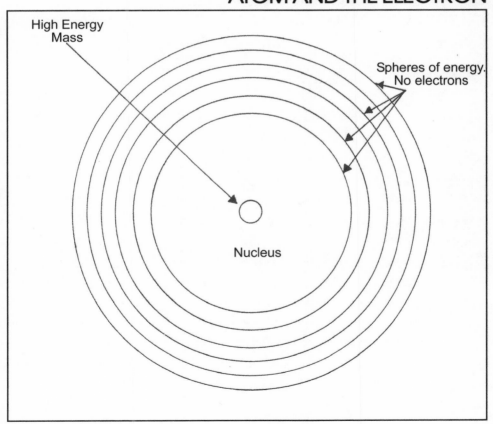

Drawing 2-1

New Theories with Interpretations

Here we see the atom, the nucleus and its spheres of energy. This is what I call Mass With Energy—MWE. Since all these spheres of energy and the nucleus are nothing but energy. The atom may be balanced with its internal energies, that is between the nucleus and the spheres of energy, but it may not be balanced with respect to its nuclear mass energies and its sphere energies.

There are no electrons in the spheres of energies of the atom. There are many spheres of energy. Each sphere has its own energy level. There is the possibility that the electron could be a form of energy between the electromagnetic spectrum and the spheres energies of the atom. See drawing.

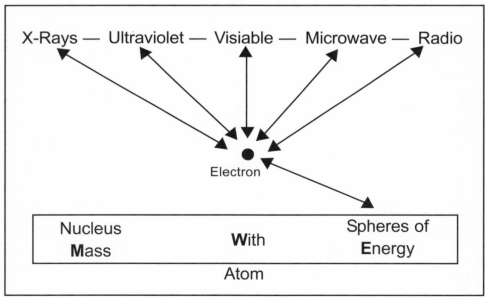

Drawing 2-2

This is only one form of action that is capable of taking place.

The electron is formed when certain changes take place with the spheres of energy. Electromagnetic spectrum energy is formed when certain changes take place with the spheres of energy.

The electromagnetic pulse energy that is formed varies in its pulse length according to which sphere of energy the electromagnetic energy pulse came from.

A moving Mass With Energy has kinetic energy. This kinetic energy is not part of the Energy of the MWE that the kinetic energy is moving.

If we move the electron, which is derived from the energy part of the MWE, we are moving a form of atomic energy.

In this case the electron does not have any of the energy of the Mass part of what I call Mass With Energy. What is the electron? In my view the electron is a form of atomic moving energy.

The electron exists only in the moving state. The electron does not exist in what we call the rest state. In the rest state the electron does not exist, it has combined with other atomic matter to assume another state.

Physics — Astronomy — Sciences
New Theories with Interpretations

Chapter 3

GALACTIC SPACE MEDIUM ENERGY—GSME.

The Galactic space medium energy is something that exists in all galactic space.

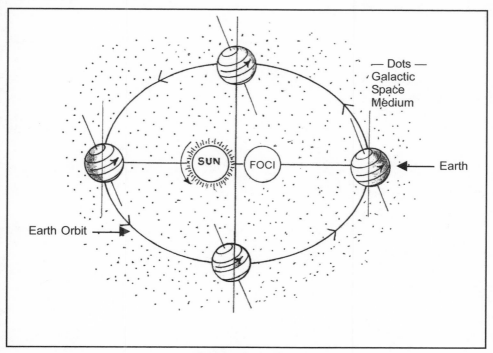

Drawing 3-1

New Theories with Interpretations

When a Mass With Energy rotates in the GSME a form of energy is introduced into the MWE. This introduced energy I call Galactic Space Medium Centrifugal Energy.

An Analogy

Galactic space medium energy	magnetism
Earth	metallic object
Rotation of Earth in galactic space medium energy	Rotation of metallic object in a magnetic field
Galactic space medium centrifugal energy	Electric current.

Drawing 3-2

This phenomenon is taking place with all planets in our galaxy.

The GSME must be something that was produced at the origin of our galaxy or is still being produced in our galaxy. Our sun also produces a GSME. Both may be the same.

CHAPTER 4

GALACTIC SPACE MEDIUM CENTRIFUGAL ENERGY — GSMCE

At the present time, 2003, rotational velocity of the earth in the Galactic Space Medium Energy is too slow to generate enough GSMCE to cause most Mass With Energy, MWE, to assume an escape velocity, except hydrogen and helium.

There is not enough GSMCE energy to produce escape velocity in the remaining MWE. Therefore, most of the GSMCE is being absorbed by the remaining MWE.

The remaining MWE with its absorbed GSMCE tries to seek its energy level on this rotating earth.

This phenomenon, a MWE with its GSMCE, will fall down if it does not have enough GSMCE. "The apple fell down." The MWE with its GSMCE, "will fall up," if it has more GSMCE. The apple fell up.

The new term "to fall up" is opposite of "to fall down".

To fall up or fall down is in reference to the rotating MWE, with its GSMCE. It is a process of seeking energy level.

This is the reason a weight, say a 1 kg MWE with its GSMCE will weigh more or weigh less at different latitudes on earth's surface, below earth's surface and at various heights above earth's surface.

There is more MWE at the equator than at the axis of rotation poles due to the fact that the earth bulges some at the equator and tapers toward the axis of rotation poles. This means that there is more MWE at the equator and less at higher latitudes moving in the GSM.

The rotation of our planetary system and rotation of the earth on its axis in the GSME produces the GSMCE.

The same weight will weigh less at the equator than at the poles.

The weight of an object is caused by GSMCE. The lack of GSMCE the more a MWE weighs.

The more GSMCE the less a MWE weighs.

Please refer to drawings 4-1, 4-2, 4-3, 4-4. Drawing 4-2 (reference) The numbers used in drawings are used only to illustrate a phenomenon.

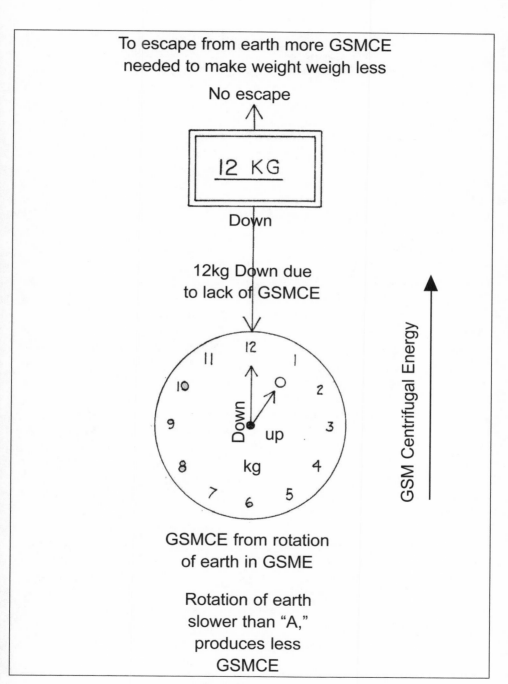

Drawing 4-1

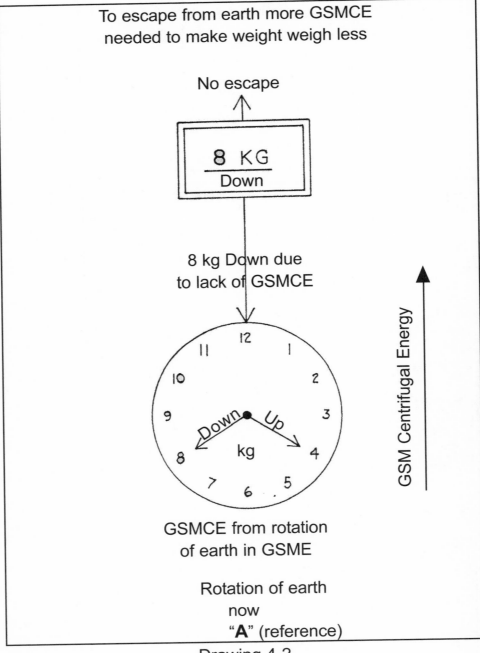

To escape from earth more GSMCE
needed to make weight weigh less

No escape

8 KG
Down

8 kg Down due
to lack of GSMCE

12
11
1
10
2
9
Down • Up
3
kg
8
4
7
6
5

GSM Centrifugal Energy

GSMCE from rotation
of earth in GSME

Rotation of earth
now
"**A**" (reference)

Drawing 4-2

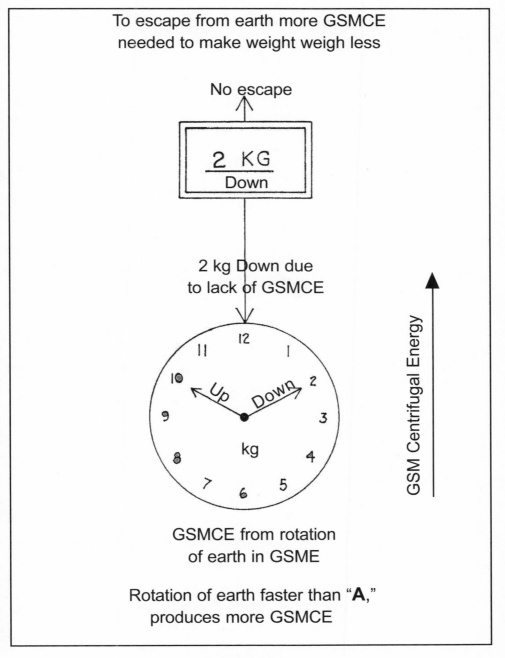

Drawing 4-3

13

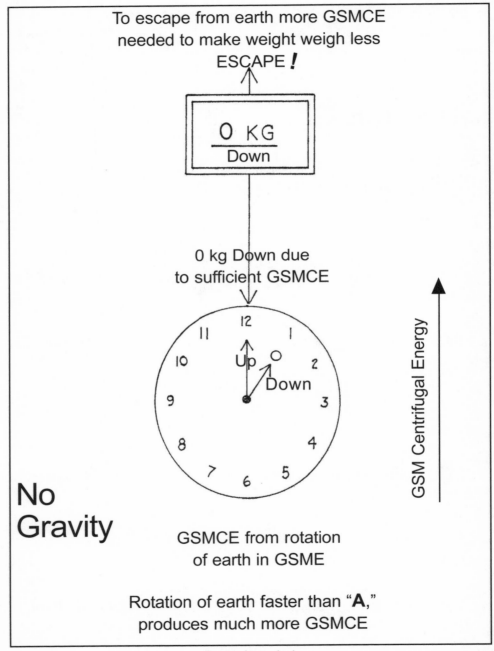

Drawing 4-4

CHAPTER 5

THEORY OF "RESONANCE ACCEPTANCE"

Everything, that is all MWE, is in a state of some degree of "resonance acceptance" with every other MWE.

All MWE that we have here on earth is made of the periodic table of elements.

Some of the man-made elements may or may not exist as part of the larger galactic system.

I am assuming that everything in all the galactic systems "hatched from the same egg".

This means that everything is related, but this does not mean that everything is the same.

We could make many speculations on this. One that I think of is that of an exploding object, as a supernova that we see or detect with instruments.

New Theories with Interpretations

There is the possibility that a supernova and similar objects could be made of 200 elements, (elements unknown to us here on earth), not just 92 as we have here on earth.

Now, from what we know about our 92 elements, think of what would happen if there were 200 elements. The weight, MWE and energy activity, would be much more than we can imagine.

We see and detect only what we are in resonance acceptance with, that is what our 92 elements are in resonance acceptance with.

Earlier I said "everything being hatched from the same egg". To me this means that everything is related by energy level. Does this mean that everything is at a different energy level, yes.

The fact that everything is at different energy levels is the reason that movement from one energy level to another energy level keeps the whole system going.

There is a continual energy exchange going on all the time. For example: Energy from the sun to earth and other planets, light energy from stars, radio energy from seen and unseen places, x-ray energy, cosmic energy, movement of planets, etc., etc.

Why would we on earth receive any of this energy or be part of this great energy exchange?

My answer to this question is "we receive these energies here on earth because of our "resonance acceptance" with these received energies".

All the MWE, being all the 92 periodic table elements, are in a varying degree of energy in "resonance acceptance" with every other periodic table element.

No matter where the energy is, it could be on earth or part of a star or galaxy.

Nothing has to be sent to the star, galaxy, sun or supernova, to say "here we are, send us your energy, light, x-rays, particles, etc., etc.". Please read my "Send-Receive Theory". Chapter 6

No, all the energies, particles, MWE, etc. are all part of the original energy package. Everything has a varying degree of energy.

This energy will transfer only to a "resonance acceptor".

It has nothing to do with the amount of energy that a sender or receiver has, it has to do with the amount of "resonance acceptance" one has for the other.

For example: let us assume a supernova is made of 200 elements and it is capable of energy transfer from 200 elements. We here on earth are only capable of receiving energies that are in resonance with our 92 elements.

So, there can be many forms of energy, from the other 108 elements. Forms of energy that we know nothing about and have no way to know whether they exist or do not exist. We have nothing in "resonance acceptance" with the 108 elements.

Now, I am sure many of you readers would like to have an example of what I am writing about.

For those of you that have some knowledge of electricity, let me explain a phenomenon of energy transfer in radio transmitting.

In a radio transmitter the final circuit before the antenna there is a coil called an inductor and a capacitor. The inductance of the coil and the capacitance of the capacitor are adjusted to the resonance frequency to be transmitted.*

The schematic circuit would look something like this.
Drawing 5-1

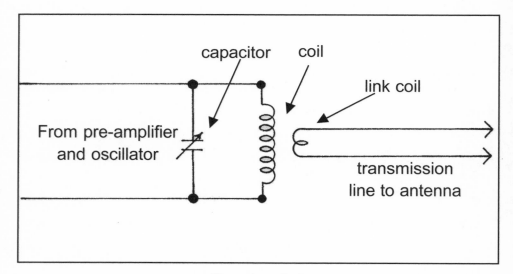

Drawing 5-1

* There is a lot more to this than what I am presenting here, but this is the basic concept.

I am presenting this to you to let you know why I use the words "resonance acceptance".

I need to explain something else before we can continue.

There is an instrument known as a "Grid-dip Oscillator". Do not let these words scare you as I will explain.

The Grid-dip Oscillator, GDO , is a small variable frequency transmitter. It also can be used as an ABSORPTION WAVEMETER. The GDO is calibrated in frequency.

In the ABSORPTION MODE THE GDO IS NOT TRANSMITTING A SIGNAL, but will absorb energy at the frequency to which it is resonated. For example: Suppose a transmitter is transmitting a signal at 7 MHz.

When the coil of the GDO, resonated to 7 MHz, is put near the coil of the transmitter, the GDO will absorb energy from transmitter transmitting a signal at 7 MHz.

If the GDO is set to 6 MHz or 8 MHz it will not absorb the 7 MHz transmitted signal of the transmitter.

The GDO will absorb energy when its resonance frequency is the same as the resonance frequency of the transmitter. See drawing 5-2

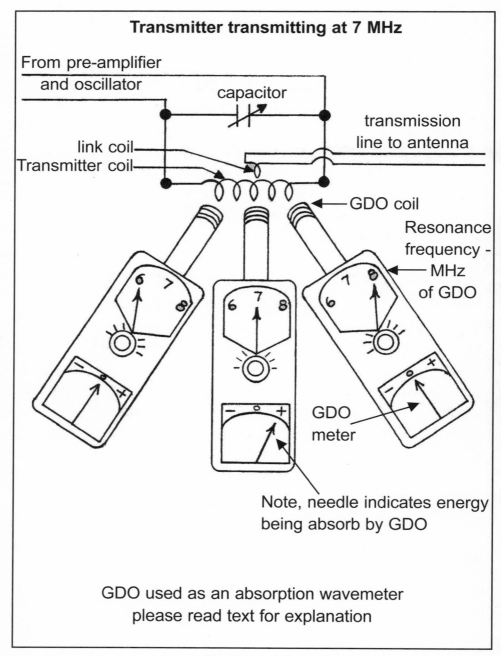

Transmitter transmitting at 7 MHz

From pre-amplifier and oscillator

capacitor

transmission line to antenna

link coil

Transmitter coil

GDO coil

Resonance frequency - MHz of GDO

GDO meter

Note, needle indicates energy being absorb by GDO

GDO used as an absorption wavemeter
please read text for explanation

Drawing 5-2

When the GDO is used as a GDO, that is it is TRANSMITTING A SIGNAL at a certain frequency—in this case a signal at 7MHz—and the coil of the GDO is put near another coil in a non-energized circuit that is also resonance at 7 MHz—then the needle on the GDO meter will "dip", indicating that energy is being removed from the GDO by the external resonance circuit.

If the GDO is transmitting a signal at 6 MHz or 8 MHz, then the non-energized 7MHz transmitter coil circuit will not absorb these signals.

See drawing 5-3 on next page

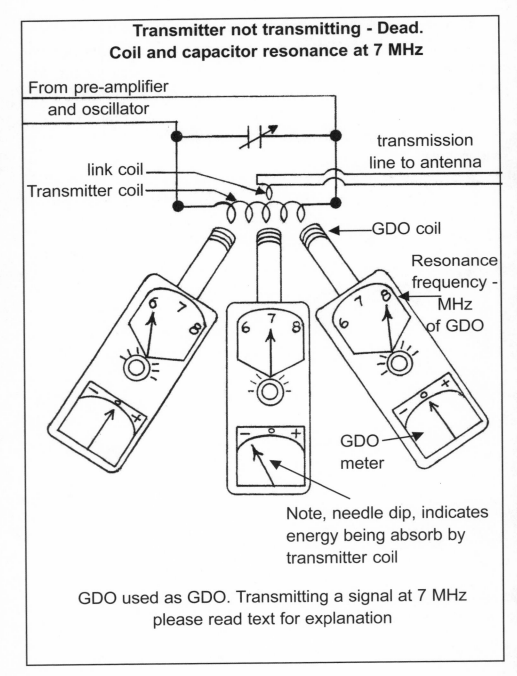

**Transmitter not transmitting - Dead.
Coil and capacitor resonance at 7 MHz**

From pre-amplifier and oscillator

transmission line to antenna

link coil
Transmitter coil

GDO coil

Resonance frequency - MHz of GDO

GDO meter

Note, needle dip, indicates energy being absorb by transmitter coil

GDO used as GDO. Transmitting a signal at 7 MHz please read text for explanation

Drawing 5-3

One more example of "resonance acceptance". Suppose a 10 watt transmitter in Hawaii is transmitting a signal at 7 MHz, and someone in Chicago, Illinois, U.S.A. wishes to receive this signal.

The person in Chicago sets his short-wave receiver to receive a 7 MHz signal. Then he connects an antenna wire to the receiver, say the wire is 150 ft in length (45.7 meters) and listens to the receiver and hears a very weak or no signal.

The signal being very weak, so the receiving antenna needs to be made resonant to the frequency of the transmitting signal, 7MHz, in Hawaii.

There is a formula for determining what the receiving antenna length should be for 7MHz. The length of the antenna should be 134 ft (40.8 meters). So the antenna wire is cut to 134 ft. and now the 7MHz signal from Hawaii is heard.

This again demonstrates "resonance acceptance".

CHAPTER 6

SEND-RECEIVE THEORY

Why does light from a distant star come to us on earth?

Why are we able to see distance or receive other electromagnetic spectrum energy?

(Please read my theory on ELECTROMAGNETIC SPECTRUM ENERGY FROM VAST DISTANCES), Chapter 10-4

Now back to the article. There must be a receiver for this energy before there can be a sender of the energy.

How does the sender know whether there is a receiver or no receiver?

Now let us see how this sending and receiving works.

Assume that there is a star that has a lot of potential energy. The star wishes to get rid of this energy before it explodes or transfoms into more MWE. So it sends out weak energy pulses of electromagnetic energy in all directions—seeking receivers to accept this energy. If there are not enough receivers for this energy, the star will start transforming to more MWE. Conversion of energy to MWE.

The weak EMS pulses go out seeking receivers for this energy, And they come upon a receiver and the receiver accepts this weak pulse.
                    Then,
this leaves an empty area where the pulse was before. Other EMS pulses move into this empty area from the same source. Soon we have a stream of EMS pulses from this specific source being accepted by this specific receiver.

A receiver can only receive that amount of energy that it is in "resonance acceptance" with the sender.

The receiver does not send out a signal to the sender, and then the sender sends a signal back to the receiver.

The earth and planets do not have enough EMS Energy to send much out to the receivers. The earth and planets are more receivers of EMS Energy than senders of EMS Energy. Unless it happened to be reflective EMS Energy, which is actually EMS Energy from another source.

Another item that I would like to present on the send-receive theory is radiation of energy from the sun.

Does the sun radiate energy equally or almost equally from all of its spherical surface?

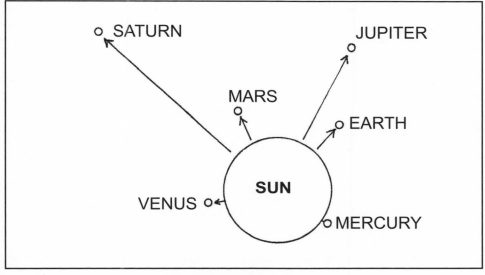

Drawing 6-1

No it does not radiate energy equally from its spherical surface.

The radiant energy will go to acceptors of the suns radiant energy. The physical size, distance and degree of resonance acceptance are all factors.

What about the sun's spherical surface areas that do not have receivers.

No receivers means no sending. There must be a receiver before there can be a sender.

So the areas of the sun's spherical surface that do not have receivers for their energy will not be able to send their energy.

In a later paper you will see that the sun has very small amount of attractive energy, but has a lot of repulsion energy.

Physics — Astronomy — Sciences
New Theories with Interpretations

CHAPTER 7

THE VOLKMANN EFFECT

MOVEMENT OF "MASS WITH ENERGY" AND ITS SELF-INDUCED BACK-FLUX RESISTANCE.

Any MWE moving in a MWE medium will have resistance to moving from the medium MWE in which it is moving.

Also, if the MWE is moving in Galactic Space Energies, the MWE will have resistance to moving. In this case, the resistance to moving is caused by a self-induced back-flux of energy produced by the moving MWE in the Galactic Space Energies.

1. We have resistance to a moving MWE when it is moving in MWE medium.

2. We also have a Back-Flux Resistance to a moving MWE caused by its movement in Galactic Space Energies. Volkmann Effect

This is a continuous on-going process for all moving MWE. There is no increase in mass of a moving MWE; there is an increase in resistances to its movement.

ENERGY VALUE LOSS IS RESISTANCE TO A MOVING MWE

Energy Value Units (EVU)

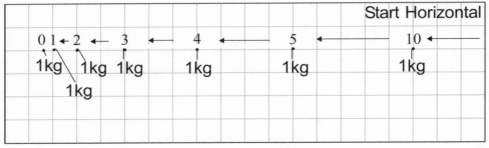

Drawing 7-1

1 kg starting with 10 EVU moves to 5 EVU. In the movement it used 5 EVU. The 1 kg is still 1 kg, but we have only 5 EVU left to move the 1 kg. Now the 5 EVU must move the 1 kg under the same conditions; so the 1 kg will not go as far this time, less energy to move the same 1 kg. This process continues until all the EVU are used.

MORE ON THE MOVING MWE BACK-FLUX ENERGY

To get a better understanding of what is to be written, it is suggested that you read chapters 19 and 20.

In order for a moving MWE to produce Back-Flux Energy, it would seem that the MWE must be moving through "something" in order to produce the Back-Flux Energy.

This "something" must exist in all galactic and extra galactic space.

What is this "something?"

We need to analyze the situation and do what we can with our present knowledge.

In Chapter 20 you will read about FORMATION ENERGY. In Chapter 20 I propose three ways that the FORMATION ENERGY could go:

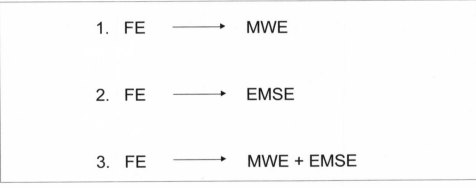

Drawing 7-2

In outer space, that is our galactic space and extra galactic space, it has been shown that there are many forms of Electromagnetic Spectrum Energies. For example: cosmic, x-ray, ultra-violet, visual, radio and others.

These Electromagnetic Spectrum Energies are coming to us, plus we, the earth and all the planets, are moving in these Galactic Space Energies.

Physics — Astronomy — Sciences
New Theories with Interpretations

> As a result of a MWE movement in the Galactic Space Energies, a Back-Flux Energy is developed that opposes movement of the MWE that caused the Back-Flux Energy to be produced. This effect is called the "Volkmann Effect."

This is similar to electrical phenomenon known as Lenz's Law. This is where an electric current flow in a wire produces its own back-flux resistance to the electric current flow. This current back-flux resistance is in addition to the wire resistance to current flow.

Do not confuse Galactic Space Medium Centrifugal Energy, GSMCE. (Chapter 4) With the Volkmann Effect.

They are two different phenomena.

CHAPTER 8

CONTRACTION OF LENGTH AND
SHRINKAGE OF A "MASS WITH ENERGY"

Note: This chapter can be very confusing, so read it with this in mind and pay close attention to details.

Developed theories on the properties of moving objects, such as the length of an object becomes shorter the faster it moves.

After studying these contraction theories, I did not think that they were correct, so I developed my own theory as to what I think takes place.

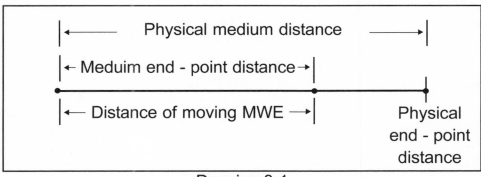

Drawing 8-1

It is not the moving MWE that shrinks, it is that the medium end-point distance is created, it being shorter with respect to the physical distance of the medium.

As you read on, you will understand this better.

The moving MWE will not go to the physical distance end-point as it does not exist for any moving MWE.

The moving MWE will not reach the physical end-point because the energy level of the moving MWE is before the physical end-point is reached.

The moving MWE energy level is at the end-point of the shortened physical end-point which is the medium end-point distance.

The shorter medium end-point exists for any moving MWE.

Where is the moving MWE medium end-point?

It is always before the physical medium end-point due to contraction of the medium distance.

There is no contraction of the moving MWE or of the medium MWE. There is only a contraction of distance.

The medium MWE end-point distance is at a lower energy level than the end-point energy level of the physical end-point distance.

Where is the missing energy?

The difference in energy level between the physical end-point distance energy level and the medium end-point distance energy level is the resistance of movement of the moving MWE in the medium MWE.

Remember, it is the distance that has contracted, not the moving MWE or the medium MWE.

Now that I have explained my theory on contraction of length of distance of a moving MWE in a medium MWE, we need to see the subject in more detail.

The physical distance end-point will now be called the imaginary end-point (the non-moving MWE end-point).

The medium distance end-point will now be called the real end-point (the moving MWE end-point).

There are two distance end-points. The imaginary distance end-point and the real distance end-point.

The non-moving MWE distance end-point is the imaginary distance end-point, in reality it does not exist. It is the distance end-point an MWE would go to if there were no resistance to the movement of the moving MWE.

The moving MWE distance end-point is the real distance end-point. In reality it does exist. It is the distance end-point an MWE does go to, because there is movement resistance to the moving MWE.

New Theories with Interpretations

The moving MWE will go to the real end-point, because the real end-point is its energy level end-point.

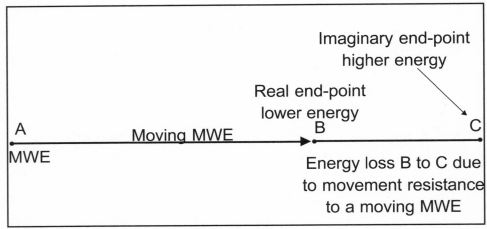

Drawing 8-2

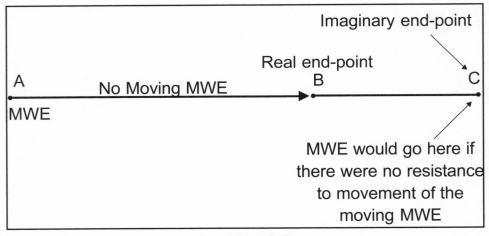

Drawing 8-3

If there is no movement of a MWE, then the imaginary distance end-point does not exist, it is only imaginary.

However, if there is movement of a MWE then the imaginary distance end-point does exist.

However, for the moving MWE the imaginary distance end-point does not exist.

Any moving MWE cannot reach its full potential due to movement resistance to a moving MWE.

If you understand what is blocked, then you understand what I am writing about.

In this article I have not included "self-induced back-flux resistance of a moving MWE", but, it too is part of the moving MWE discussed above. Volkmann Effect.

Please read my article "Movement of Mass With Energy and Its Self-Induced Back-Flux Resistance - Volkmann Effect." Chapter 7

Physics — Astronomy — Sciences
New Theories with Interpretations

CHAPTER 9

CONTRACTION OF THE CIRCUMFERENCE OF A ROTATING "MASS WITH ENERGY."

Just as there is contraction of distance for a linear moving MWE, there, also is contraction of a circumference, or any non-linear moving MWE or any curved MWE movement. For example: a planet rotating around the sun. A rotating MWE, in this case a planet, moving in interstellar matter and galactic space energies.

The rotating MWE does not shrink in size or contract in length due to this effect. It is the circumference distance that is shortened.

In this case we have a counter clockwise Elliptical Spiral with an ever decreasing circumference.

(Please read my paper "Contraction of Length. And Shrinkage of a MWE," chapter 8.

The planet or planets will eventually move into the sun to provide fuel for the solar engine, MAYBE! It all depends on energy values. Please read my papers "Attraction Energy Value of the Nine Planets and the Sun" chapter 17-2 and "Repulsion Energy Value Of The Sun." chapter 17-3.

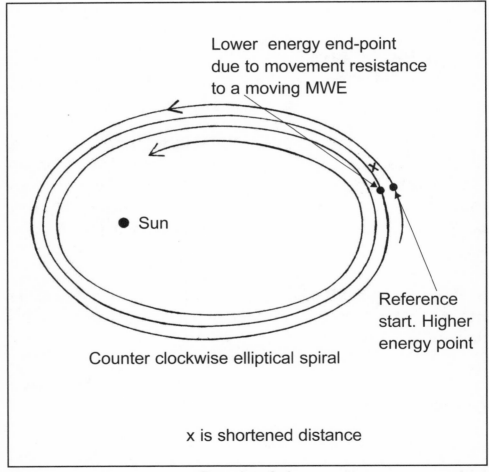

Drawing 9-1

The shortened distance "X" is also the amount of energy value change due to movement resistance.

If the situation were reversed, the planet rotating about the sun faster, then the clockwise elliptical spiral circumference would become greater. In this case, the gained energy could be called "Elliptical Centrifugal Energy".

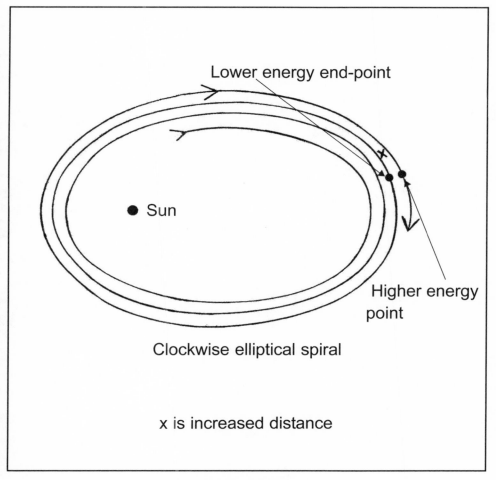

Lower energy end-point

● Sun

Higher energy point

Clockwise elliptical spiral

x is increased distance

Drawing 9-2

Physics — Astronomy — Sciences
New Theories with Interpretations

Please read my papers "Movement of a Mass With Energy and its Self-Induced Back-Flux Resistance" Volkmann Effect, chapter 7, and "Our Sun, Repulsion Energy and Attraction Energy," chapter 18.

CHAPTER 10 PART 1

ELECTROMAGNETIC SPECTRUM AS IT IS NOW

Present information on the electromagnetic spectrum shows that the electromagnetic spectrum is composed of many frequencies that are sinusoidal wave form, that is the wave starts at zero, goes to peak, back to zero, back to peak, back to zero. This looks like a type of electric sine wave produced by a coil of wire rotating in a magnetic field.

In 1775 the Danish Astronomer, Roemer, determined the speed of light. His method determined how long it took light to travel the major axis of the earth's orbit.

The sun's spectrum as seen on earth peaks around 500nm. The human eye for scotopic vision (low light and night vision) also peaks around 500 nm.

The light seen by Roemer must have been mostly around 500 nm, so it would seem that the light he saw was in this 500 nm region, therefore, the speed of the EMS light pulse he saw was for this pulse length, 500 nm, 500×10^{-9} meters. This being

New Theories with Interpretations

based on the speed of light being around 3.0×10^8 meters/second.

In the following two Drawings (10-1) 1 and (10-1) 2, one can see the way the electromagnetic system is now. Any number of cycles per second. 1000 Hz/sec., 10,000 Hz/sec., 100,000Hz/sec., etc. The second is the time base.

The system is based on the time unit of one second. The number of wavelengths per second.

There are actually two, three and maybe more speeds to the EMS in my theory.

The first speed in my theory is the pulse as a unit. This is the time-distance that it takes from start of a pulse to the end of the pulse.

The second speed in my theory is the speed of this completed pulse As A Unit in a vacuum. More on this later.

In modern day Physics these two speeds are considered to be the same, one speed.

THE WAY IT IS NOW. ANY NUMBER OF Hz / Sec.

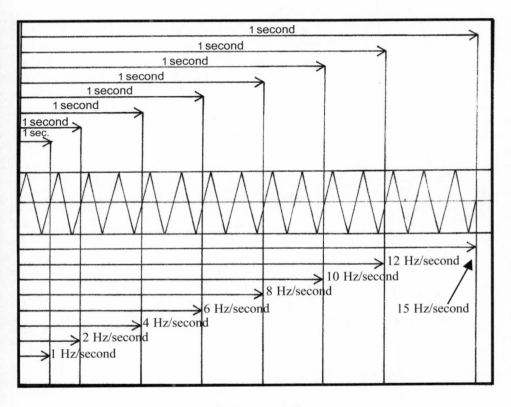

Drawing (10-1) 1

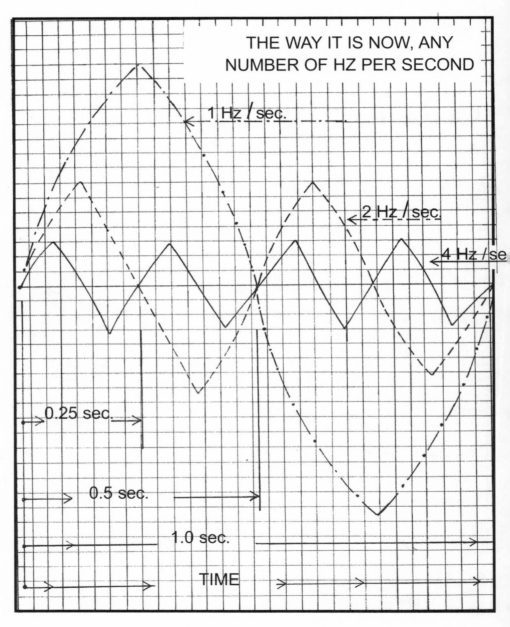

Drawing (10-1) 2

CHAPTER 10   PART 2

BASIC INFORMATION ON ELECTROMAGNETIC SPECTRUM PULSES:

For text reference please refer to drawing (10-2) 1

More on my theories. Pulse length speed, m/s, is the speed of the pulse length.

This pulse length speed, m/s, is the same for every pulse length.

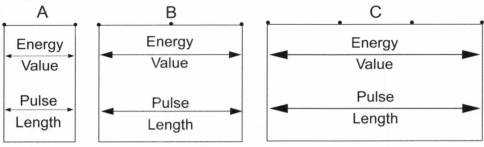

Drawing (10-2) 1

Each pulse has a different length.
Each pulse length has the same energy value.
Each pulse length has the same speed, m/s.

From the above we can say— a short pulse as "A" above has all its energy in a short length. A long pulse as "C" above has all its energy in a longer length. All three lengths "A", "B", "C", each have the same energy value.

I hope that you understand the above, because now we have another speed. Pulse length As A Unit (AAU) speed. The pulse length speed As A Unit (AAU)—that is the pulse length speed As A Unit (AAU) length, "A" length, "B" length or "C" length all have the same speed in a vacuum.

There is also another pulse speed which you will read about later. It involves the speed in a transparent Mass With Energy medium.

CHAPTER 10   PART 3

THE ELECTROMAGNETIC SPECTRUM- EMS

The Physics books state that all the various wave lengths that make up the electromagnetic spectrum move at the same speed in a vacuum.

First, when we use the terms wave length and wave, just what type of wave are we speaking of. I think most Physicists would think of the usual sine wave type. My belief is that the EMS is not made of waves of energy, but pulses of energy.

The EMS pulses are pulses of many lengths. The pulses are of equal energy value for their entire length; also the pulse length time is different for each pulse, and the PULSE LENGTH AS A UNIT movement time in a vacuum is the same for all PULSE LENGTHS AS A UNIT. This is what we now call the speed of light.

FOR TEXT REFERENCE PLEASE REFER TO DRAWING (10-3) 1

After you have studied the chart to understand it, you will see how 10 pulses of different pulse lengths, all starting at the same zero-point, end. After 10 pulses of R, which is R 10, which arrives at the recording instrument before the tenth pulse of o, y, g, b, i and v arrive to the recording instrument.

The recording instrument will receive 10 pulses of R before it receives any of the other pulses.

In fact, none of the shorter length pulses will ever catch up with the longer length pulses that they started with.

Also, notice that the energy value of each EMS energy pulse is always the same. Short pulse length or long pulse length.

For example: R to R1, R1 to R2, R2 to R3, etc. are all the same energy value and the energy value R to R1 and the energy value V to V1 are the same. It is the length that changes, not the energy value. As stated earlier, each EMS pulse is a pulse of a certain length and of equal energy value for its entire length.

The electromagnetic spectrum pulse length pulses do not have a self-producing back-flux resistance by their movement. A Mass With Energy has a back-flux resistance by its movement. Volkmann Effect.

Because the electromagnetic spectrum pulses do not produce a back-flux resistance is the reason EMS pulse length pulses can move vast distances. The EMS pulse length pulses can move on and on and on.

The only resistance to their movement is when they encounter a MWE and are absorbed or reflected or the SPEED of the pulse length pulse As A Unit (AAU) changes (not the speed of the individual pulse length) by back-flux of the transport medium. More on this later.

For drawing (10-3) 1 please see following fold-out page.

CHAPTER 10   PART 4

ELECTROMAGNETIC SPECTRUM ENERGY FROM VAST DISTANCES

The movement of an electromagnetic spectrum pulse length AAU does not produce a back-flux resistance or have contraction of length, because it has no mass, just energy.

The electromagnetic pulse length pulses without a carrier can move on and on and on. Since electromagnetic energy needs no carrier and produces no self resistance (back-flux resistance) Volkmann Effect.

This is the reason electromagnetic pulse length pulses can move vast distances. Examples: light energy, x-ray energy, radio energy, etc. All from vast distances.

The only resistances to a moving electromagnetic spectrum pulse length pulse is a resonance acceptor, such as a Mass With Energy or any other influence that would cause a back-flux (Volkmann Effect) to take place, with its influence on the pulse length As A Unit (AAU) speed. Not on the individual pulse length speed itself.

CHAPTER 10   PART 5

ELECTROMAGNETIC SPECTRUM PULSE SPEED AAU IN A TRANSPARENT MWE MEDIUM

Speed of an EMS energy pulse AAU as it goes though a piece of clear glass. (MWE MEDIUM)

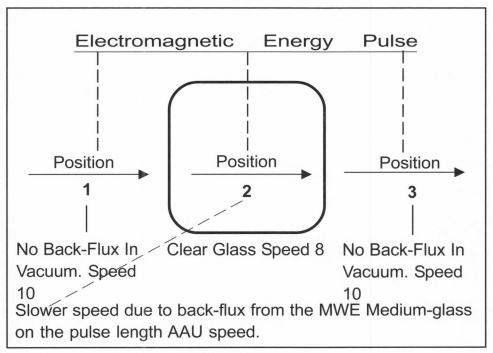

Drawing (10-5) 1

New Theories with Interpretations

The numbers 10 and 8 are used to illustrate a point. The EMS pulse length speed, the EMS pulse length and the EMS energy valve all remain the same. It is the speed of the EMS pulse length speed As A Unit (AAU) that changes.

CHAPTER 10 PART 6

ELECTROMAGNETIC SPECTRUM SPEEDS

There are three speed times in my new electromagnetic spectrum pulse theory:

For Text reference Please refer to drawing (10-6) 1

1. Speed time of a pulse length is the time required for a pulse's length to form. This is the pulse length speed time.

2. Speed time of a PULSE LENGTH AS A UNIT in a vacuum is the speed time of a PULSE LENGTH AS A UNIT in its movement in a vacuum. This is what we now refer to as the speed of light.

3. PULSE LENGTH SPEED TIME and PULSE LENGTH SPEED TIME AS A UNIT in a Mass With Energy medium. Please see Chapter 10 Part 5 "The EMS Pulse Speed AAU In A Transparent MWE Medium".

The electromagnetic spectrum pulse length is the determining factor for all the differences in the electromagnetic pulses, from x-ray pulses to radio pulses, etc.

There is another factor that is THE VERY BASIC ENERGY VALUE OF THE EMS PULSE. Since all pulses have the same energy value.

This suggests that there is a basic fundamental energy value for all EMS pulses: x-ray, ultra-violet, light, radio, etc.

What is this fundamental energy value for all EMS pulses?

The pulse length energy value could be called the basic pulse energy value for the electromagnetic spectrum pulses.

We still have more to investigate, moving distances of the Mass With Energy and the electromagnetic spectrum energy moving distances. If a carrier is used to transport the electromagnetic spectrum pulse length pulses, the MWE carrier medium causes a back-flux energy to develop which opposes the EMS PULSE LENGTH SPEED AS A UNIT, Thereby causing the EMS PULSE LENGTH AS A UNIT to move at a slower speed. This action DOES NOT effect the pulse length, or the pulse length speed. ONLY THE SPEED OF THE PULSE LENGTH AS A UNIT.

Every electromagnetic system energy pulse has its own pulse forming distance-time. This determines the pulse length. Remember all EMS pulses have the same energy value. The energy value is the same for any length of EMS pulse. All electromagnetic energy pulses are of the same energy value even though their length may be different.

The SPEED of the EMS energy pulse length As A Unit (AAU) can change. Its speed depends on the medium in which it is being transported.

The speed of the EMS energy pulse As A Unit (AAU) can change, but the pulse length remains the same and the energy value of the pulse length remains the same.

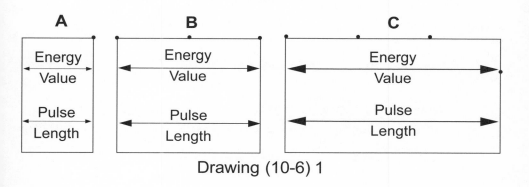

Drawing (10-6) 1

One more bit of information.

An x-ray pulse of 3×10^{-8} cm length has the same energy value as a radio pulse of 6×10^4 cm.

Here we can see that the short length x-ray pulse has a tremendous amount of energy in a short length pulse compared to a long length radio pulse.

Both have the same energy value, but different lengths.

Remember that pulse length speed is not the same a pulse length speed As A Unit, (AAU).

New Theories with Interpretations

In today's electromagnetic theory the term wave length is used most of the time instead of pulse and the speed of the wave length and the speed of the wave length As A Unit are the same in a vacuum.

In my theory, there are three speeds for the pulse:

1. Pulse length speed time, which is different for each pulse length, provided they are not the same length.

2. Pulse length speed time As a Unit (AAU) in a vacuum.

3. Pulse length speed time As A Unit (AAU) in a Mass With Energy (MWE) medium. Please read part 5 of chapter 10. "EMS Pulse Speed AAU In A Transparent Medium."

CHAPTER 11

FLOW OF ELECTRICITY—FLOW OF ELECTRONS OR FLOW OF MAGNETISM ?

The Flow of what we call electricity may not be what it is said to be, a "flow of electrons".

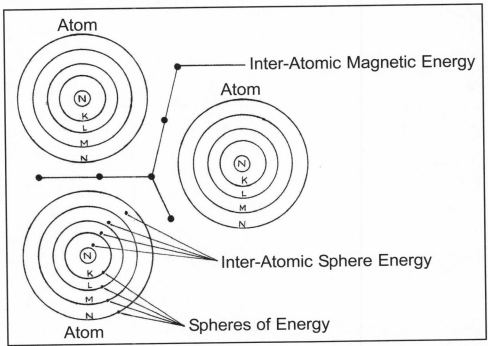

Drawing 11-1

It is a flow of magnetism, a special type of magnetism I call "inter atomic magnetic energy".

There are no electrons outside the nucleus. The orbits are really spheres of energy.

Electrons are produced when there is a change in energy value among the spheres of energy causing a transformation of energy to form an electron or electromagnetic energy or both.

For an example, lets illustrate the flow of Inter-Atomic-Magnetic-Energy from a generator to a motor.

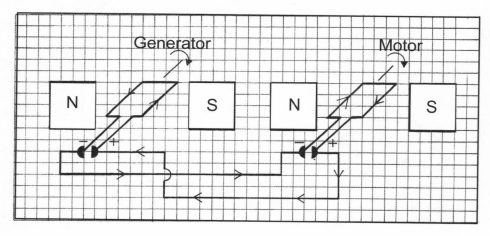

Drawing 11-2

Assume we have a copper wire coil (armature) rotating in a magnetic energy field.

Rotation of the armature in the magnetic energy field causes the "Inter-Atomic-Magnetic-Energy" to move.

At the point of inception the "Inter-Atomic-Magnetic-Energy" level will be higher than the surrounding Inter-Atomic-Magnetic-Energy level, so the Inter-Atomic-Magnetic-Energy will move into this lover level.

As the rotation of the armature increases, more and more, it causes an increase of Inter-Atomic-Magnetic-Energy level.

This continuation of increase in Inter-Atomic-Magnetic-Energy level at point of inception causes the Inter-Atomic-Magnetic-Energy pressure to flow in the wire from high value to lower value.

At the far end of the wire the Inter-Atomic-Magnetic-Energy enters a coil in a magnetic field.

The Inter-Atomic-Magnetic-Energy causes a magnetic field to build up in the coil. This coil field will oppose or add to the existing pole field causing the coil to rotate.

Was the flow of what we call electricity achieved by the flow of electrons or by the flow of magnetism?

Before closing this chapter we need to consider the fact that there may be more than one type of electricity.

The magnetic flow type and an electron flow type produced by ionization as caused by chemical action—batteries.

If the two types of electricity do exist, then we need to develop instruments that will differentiate between the two.

New Theories with Interpretations

If there are two or more types of electricity and we as scientists are able to separate them, then there would be the greatest economic period the world has ever seen.

This would be a good PhD project for some of you young scientists.

CHAPTER 12

WILL AN OBJECT—A MASS WITH ENERGY— LAUNCHED INTO SPACE EVER STOP ?

A MWE launched in the direction of earth's rotation will have the earth's west to east rotational energy plus the launch energy.

Since the space medium is not very conductive to receiving the two energies, mentioned above, the moving MWE could go in space forever.

However, the moving MWE WILL NOT go traveling forever. There is another factor to consider. That is the Volkmann Effect. It is known as Back-Flux Resistance of a moving MWE. This will finally bring the moving MWE to a stop. Please read my paper "MOVEMENT OF A MASS WITH ENERGY AND ITS SELF-INDUCED BACK-FLUX RESISTANCE—VOLKMANN EFFECT" chapter 7.

All of the launched energy and energy from earth's rotation, west to east will have been canceled by the self—produced Back-Flux Resistance, little by little as it moves through space, to the point where there is no motion energy left.

New Theories with Interpretations

Remember there are two resistances to this movement
1. Energy value loss is a resistance
2. Back-Flux Energy is a resistance

Energy value loss is a form of resistance

The loss of energy value from a moving MWE means that the remaining energy value has to move the same amount of MWE with less energy. Therefore, energy value loss is a resistance to movement.

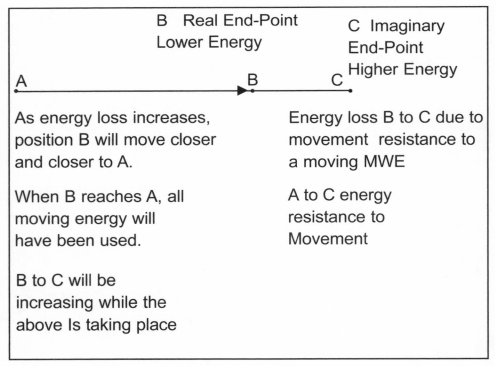

B   Real End-Point
Lower Energy

C Imaginary
End-Point
Higher Energy

A ———————————————→ B   C

As energy loss increases, position B will move closer and closer to A.

When B reaches A, all moving energy will have been used.

B to C will be increasing while the above Is taking place

Energy loss B to C due to movement resistance to a moving MWE

A to C energy resistance to Movement

Drawing 12-1

In this case the Back-Flux Energy causes the MWE movement to slow. The Back-Flux Energy slowly neutralizes the forward MWE Movement Energy.

Now what happens to the MWE when its movement energy becomes zero?

What I think will happen is the "dead" MWE will become the captive of the nearest space energy flux.

Please read my paper 'CONTRACTION OF LENGTH AND SHRINKAGE OF A MASS WITH ENERGY" chapter 8.

CHAPTER 13

A VERTICAL ASSIST OBJECT FROM EARTH'S SURFACE

In the drawing we see the elliptical orbit of a VERTICAL launched object from surface of earth.

Please refer to the drawing for details

The 1 Kg object retains its initial eastward ground speed as it moves up and down. Each latitude has its own rotational speed.

The speed will be fast at launch point and at impact point.

The speed will be slow at both aprogees. There are no perigees, unless one wishes to use launch point and impact point as perigees.

Now, this is just the opposite from what happens with an elliptical orbit of a planet around the sun.

The object I am writing about is launched at the end of the minor axis at its intersection with the ellipse orbit.

The elliptical orbit of a Vertical launched object from surface of earth

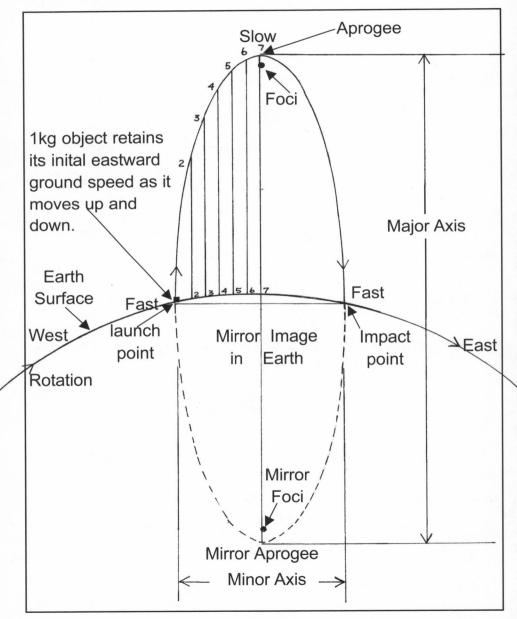

Drawing 13-1

CHAPTER 14

DOPPLER EFFECT

The reason for this chapter is that I want to present my interpretation of the doppler effect.

For example: using a moving 330 Hz/sec. signal pressure movement in air.

This is the frequency the stationary listener will hear when the 330 Hz/sec. is not moving.

Now, if the 330 Hz/sec. signal is moving toward the stationary listener—the stationary listener will hear the 330 Hz/sec. signal more times per second. Not at a higher frequency than the 330 Hz/sec. signal.

Ask yourself the question, why should the 330 Hz/sec. signal change its frequency just because it is moving?

If the signal is approaching the stationary listener—the 330 Hz/sec. signal will be heard more times per second by the stationary listener.

New Theories with Interpretations

If the signal is receding from the stationary listener—the 330 HZ/sec. will be heard less times per second by the stationary listener.

The signal carrier moving forward or backward is not going to change the original frequency signal.

On the chart, I have put the stationary observer and the signals energies accumulation barrier at the end of the 4th second, although I could have stopped sooner or extended the chart.

Notice all signals movements energies accumulate at the same time at the end of the 4th second where I put the signals energies accumulation barrier.

As the moving time - distance, from the start, is extended, the signals energies accumulation barrier accumulates more and more energy.

If the amount of energy accumulated in the accumulation barrier is more than the medium that the energy is moving in can absorb, then the accumulated energies will be more than the medium can absorb and we have the sonic boom.

The stationary observer and the end of the 4th second received four 330 HZ/sec. signals at the same time, not just one 330 Hz/sec. signal as it would be if the 330 Hz/sec. signal were not moving.

Notice that the 330 Hz/sec. signal energy starts to accumulate after "start" to end of the 4th second.

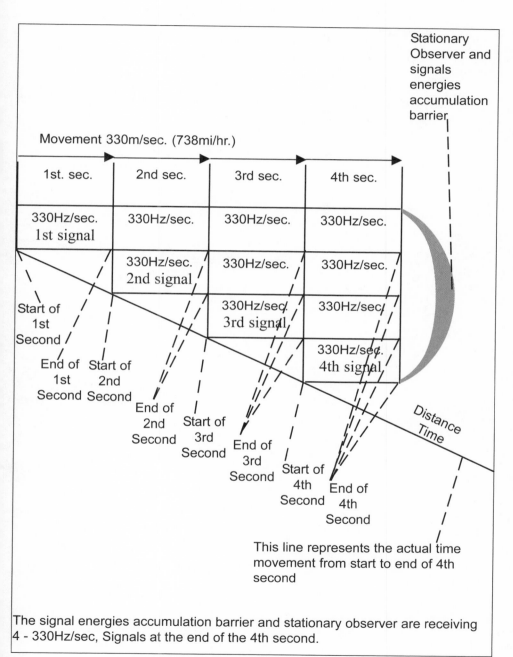

Drawing 14-1

Actually the time I used, 4 seconds, may be broken down into any number of smaller time units.

During the entire process there is no change in frequency of the 330 Hz/sec. signal.

CHAPTER 15

DISTANCE AND TIME, ARE THEY THE SAME?

Are distance and time the same or are they different?

Now, let me explain my views on distance and time.

On distance, we have fixed distance and moving distance. Fixed distance is measured distance here on earth. That is, a person measures distance on earth with his measuring tools.

If the distance on earth between x and y is 160 meters, the distance is a fixed distance. A person can walk or run the distance and it is still 160 meters. The earth rotates on its axis and in its orbit about the sun, the distance between x and y is still the same 160 meters, this is a fixed distance.

Moving distances are the moving earth, planets, sun, stars, galaxies, etc. These objects are constantly changing distances among themselves.

Physics — Astronomy — Sciences
New Theories with Interpretations

Most actions, particle movement, chemical reactions, clock time, life, etc., are usually distance-time movement. That is, they are measured to the earth's rotation on its axis or earth's orbit around the sun.

Example: If a person lives 72 years—time— what we mean is he has lived a distance of 72 orbits—distance—of the earth around the sun.

Are time and distance the same, or just different names for the same phenomena?

On fixed time, the meter length, here on earth, is still the same distance after 72 orbits around the sun. The time or distance involved did not change the meter length on earth.

For Mass With Energy movement measurements we use fixed earth distances.

There is also electromagnetic spectrum movement distances. Here we use a fixed earth distance for measurement of an electromagnetic spectrum pulse distance. This is not the best way, but at the present time we have no other way.

Mass With Energy and the electromagnetic spectrum are two entirely different systems.

A fixed distance here on earth can be measured with our measuring devices, fixed distances involve Mass With Energy. When a fixed distance involves movement we usually use earth's rotation on its axis and/or rotation around the sun as a reference.

However, when there is movement of electromagnetic spectrum energy, we come upon new problems. Are we going to use fixed distance measuring methods to measure fast moving electromagnetic spectrum energy? That is what we do now.

How does one go about measuring electromagnetic energy distance movement without using fixed distance methods?

The problem is that we have moving electromagnetic spectrum energy distances, and with this we have to deal with an uncertainty. That is everything is moving at different speeds, at different distances, and at different distance-times.

CHAPTER 16

ENERGY AND OUR GALACTIC AND EXTRA GALACTIC ENERGY

Now we need to study our galactic and extra galactic space energy and energy in general.

There are many forms of energy in our galactic and extra galactic systems.

Everything is in some form of energy. Motion is the movement of energy from one energy level to another energy level.

Many forms of our galactic and extra galactic space energy have been discovered in the last 100 years.

Some examples:

In 1931 amateur radio scientist W8JK, Karl Jansky, discovered radio signals coming from the Milky Way.

New Theories with Interpretations

In 1937 amateur radio scientist W9GFZ, Grote Reber, made a 9 meter parabolic dish antenna for the study of galactic space energy. In 1941 he published the first radio energy map of the sky.

These two amateur radio scientists started radio astronomy.

More of our galactic and extra galactic energy discoveries are: solar wind, magnetic fields on the sun, our galactic and   extra galactic magnetic field sources, ionized gas in the upper atmosphere, x-rays from outer space, cosmic rays from outer space, microwave cosmic radiation and others.

Our galactic and extra galactic energy sources have been discovered in the past 100 years. I believe more types of our galactic and extra galactic energy will be discovered in the future. So you can see that there is a lot of research to be done. We have just started.

After much thinking, reading and writing, I wonder about what we call energy. We can say that there are many forms of energy, but do we know what energy is? It seems to be the belief that what we call energy goes from what we say is a high energy level to a low energy level, and it seems to be that way.

If all energy seems to be going from a high level to a low level, then we could say that at some time all energy would be at a level at which there would be no high energy left to go to a low energy level.

What is this level?

The lowest energy level that is possible is when there is no Mass With Energy left for energy to move into or out of. At this state, all the Mass With Energy has been converted to Electromagnetic energy and there is no Mass With Energy left.

Which way is the whole system going? Is it going to a more Mass With Energy state, or is it going to an all energy state?

On these questions, I would say that we do not know the answers, but the system seems to be going to a state of condensed energy, that is the system is going to more MWE.

CHAPTER **17**   PART 1

GRAVITY *!* WHAT GRAVITY *?*

If gravity existed as now explained, all the planets would have been already drawn into the sun.

According to today's gravity theory
1. Gravity is an attractive force
2. Two objects at rest will attract each other

In order for two objects to attract each other and thereby move toward each other, they must have some type of energy within themselves to make this attraction movement take place. Without this attractive energy, the objects at rest will not move together.

Before getting into my theory you will need to read my paper entitled "Energy and Our Galactic and Extra Galactic Energy" Chapter 16.

Now let us look into some known phenomena and work our way to my theory.

Two parallel wires carrying electric currents in the same direction attract each other.

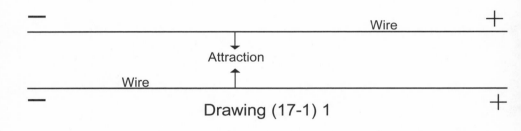

Drawing (17-1) 1

Two parallel wires carrying electric currents in the opposite directions repel each other

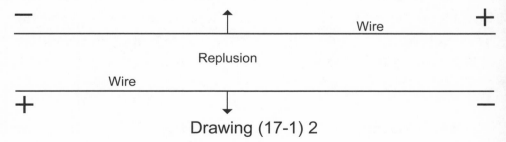

Drawing (17-1) 2

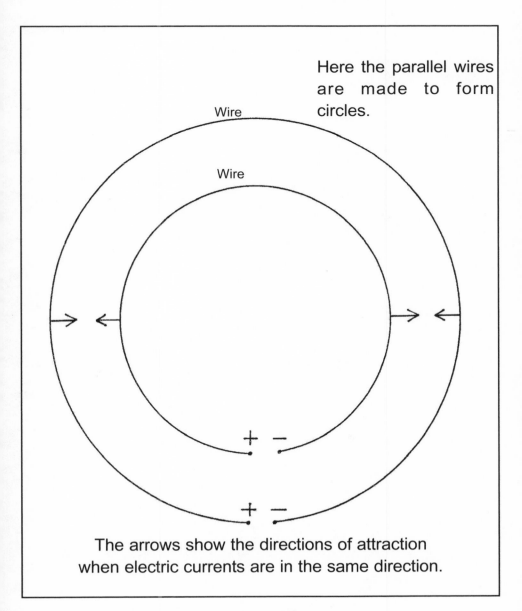

Here the parallel wires are made to form circles.

Wire

Wire

The arrows show the directions of attraction when electric currents are in the same direction.

Drawing (17-1) 3

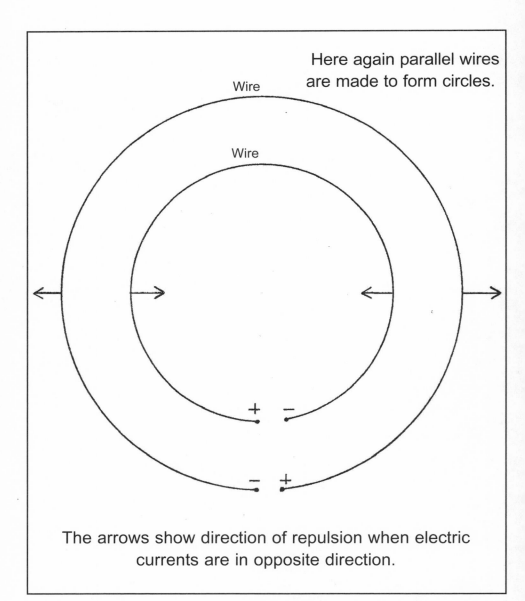

Here again parallel wires are made to form circles.

Wire

Wire

The arrows show direction of repulsion when electric currents are in opposite direction.

Drawing (17-1) 4

Now lets condense the wires so each wire becomes one lump of material. Each lump of material goes in its own elliptical orbit. These lumps of material we will call planets. P1 being Earth and P2 being Mars.

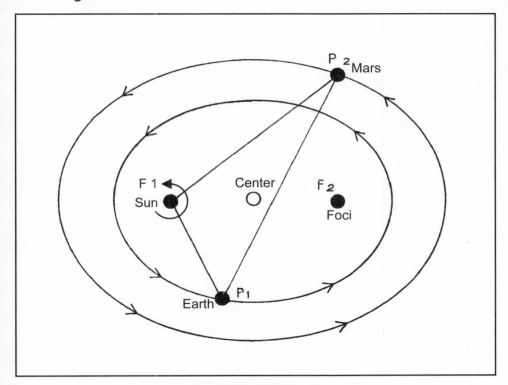

Drawing (17-1) 5

These two planets will do to illustrate how the planets and sun attract. Notice all are moving in a counter clockwise direction.

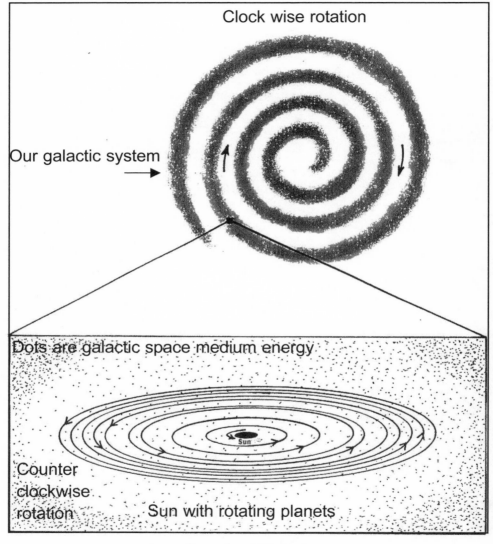

Clock wise rotation

Our galactic system

Dots are galactic space medium energy

Sun

Counter clockwise rotation

Sun with rotating planets

Drawing(17-1) 6

Our solar system "shown in the blocked area," moves clockwise in our galactic system.

The planets move through our galactic space energy while going in their elliptical orbits about the sun. While this is taking place, our solar system is also moving clockwise in our galaxy.

Where does this Galactic Space Medium Energy (GSME) come from?

My thinking is that this GSME our sun and planets are moving in is part of our galactic system.

The movements that we are concerned with are
1. Counter clockwise movement of our sun and planets in our solar system.
2. Clockwise movement of our solar system in our galaxy.

In the enclosed box is our solar system, sun and planets with the dots representing our Galactic Space Medium Energy.

Please read chapter 4 "Galactic Space Medium Centrifugal Energy.

CHAPTER 17 PART 2

ATTRACTION ENERGY VALUE OF THE NINE PLANETS AND THE SUN

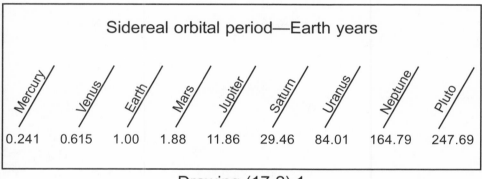

Drawing (17-2) 1

$$\frac{247.69 \ \text{Pluto}}{0.241 \ \text{Mercury}} = $$ 1,027.76 number of times Mercury will orbit the sun during Pluto's orbit.

$$\frac{247.69 \ \text{Pluto}}{0.615 \ \text{Venus}} = $$ 402.75 number of times Venus will orbit the sun during Pluto's orbit.

$$\frac{247.69 \ \text{Pluto}}{1.00 \ \text{Earth}} = $$ 247.69 number of times Earth will orbit the sun during Pluto's orbit

New Theories with Interpretations

$$\frac{247.69 \text{ Pluto}}{1.88 \text{ Mars}} = \quad \text{131.75 number of times Mars will orbit the sun during Pluto's orbit}$$

$$\frac{247.69 \text{ Pluto}}{11.86 \text{ Jupiter}} = \quad \text{20.88 number of times Jupiter will orbit the sun during Pluto's orbit}$$

$$\frac{247.69 \text{ Pluto}}{29.46 \text{ Saturn}} = \quad \text{8.41 number of times Saturn will orbit the sun during Pluto's orbit}$$

$$\frac{247.69 \text{ Pluto}}{84.01 \text{ Uranus}} = \quad \text{2.95 number of times Uranus will orbit the sun during Pluto's orbit}$$

$$\frac{247.69 \text{ Pluto}}{164.79 \text{ Neptune}} = \quad \text{1.50 number of times Neptune will orbit the sun during Pluto's orbit}$$

$$\frac{247.69 \text{ Pluto}}{247.69 \text{ Pluto}} = \quad \text{1.00 number of times Pluto will orbit the sun during Pluto's orbit}$$

The above chart shows the number of times each planet orbits the sun compared to the orbital period of Pluto.

Pluto having the longest orbital time distance in years. We need to find the attractive energy value for each planet, so we can get the total attractive energy valve for our solar system. For example: Mercury will make 1027.76 orbits about the sun while Pluto makes 1 orbit about the sun.

Now we need to take the Mass (MWE) of each planet and multiply this by the number of times each planet orbits the sun compared to the orbital period of Pluto.

Mass (MWE) X Number of times planet   =   Attractive energy
               will orbit the sun during   value kg/247.69
               Pluto's orbit   earth years

Mercury
$3,300 \times 10^{20}$ kg $\times 1,027.76 = 3,391,608 \times 10^{20}$ kg/247.69 years

Venus
$48,700 \times 10^{20}$ kg $\times 402.75 = 19,613,925 \times 10^{20}$ kg/247.69 years

Earth
$59,700 \times 10^{20}$ kg $\times 247.69 = 14,787,093 \times 10^{20}$ kg/247.69 years

Mars
$6,420 \times 10^{20}$ kg $\times 131.75 = 845,835 \times 10^{20}$ kg/247.69 years

Jupiter
$18,990,000 \times 10^{20}$ kg $\times 20.88 = 396,511,200 \times 10^{20}$ kg/247.69 years

Saturn
$5,680,000 \times 10^{20}$ kg $\times 8.41 = 47,768,800 \times 10^{20}$ kg/247.69 years

Uranus
$868,000 \times 10^{20}$ kg $\times 2.95 = 2,560.6 \times 10^{20}$ kg/247.69 years

Neptune
$1,020,000 \times 10^{20}$ kg $\times 1.50 = 1,530,000 \times 10^{20}$ kg/247.69 years

Pluto
125×10^{20} kg $\times 1 = 125 \times 10^{20}$ kg/247.69 years

Attractive Energy Value

Mercury - - - - - - - - - - -3,391,608 x 10^{20} kg

Venus - - - - - - - - - - 19,613,925 x 10^{20} kg

Earth - - - - - - - - - - 14,787,093 x 10^{20} kg

Mars - - - - - - - - - - - -845,835 x 10^{20} kg

Jupiter - - - - - - - - - -396,511,200 x 10^{20} kg

Saturn - - - - - - - - - - 47,768,800 x 10^{20} kg

Uranus - - - - - - - - - - - - -2,561 x 10^{20} kg

Neptune - - - - - - - - - - -1,530,000 x 10^{20} kg

Pluto - - - - - - - - - - - - - - -125 x 10^{20} kg

Total 484,451,022 x 10^{20} kg/247.69 earth years

Or

0.0484451022 x 10^{30} kg/247.69 earth years

This is the ATTRACTIVE VALUE FOR THE NINE PLANETS. Not much.

ATTRACTIVE VALUE FOR THE SUN IS 4,973 x 10^{30} kg/247.69 earth years

Attractive Energy Value For Our Sun

Sun Orbital Period in Years

The sun roates once on its axis every 36 earth days, counterclockwise.

$$\frac{36 \text{ earth days—sun rotation on its axis}}{365 \text{ earth days—earth rotation years}}$$ on its axis for 1 year. $= 0.0986$ years, sun rotation on its axis in earth years.

Pluto Orbital Period

$$\frac{247.69 \text{ Pluto}}{0.0986 \text{ Sun}} \quad = \quad 2,512.06$$
sun rotation on its   Number of times
axis in earth years   the sun will rotate
                        on its axis during
                        Pluto's orbit

Mass of sun **x** number of times the sun will rotate on its axis during Pluto's orbit

1.98×10^{30} kg **x** $2,512.06 = 4,973.878 \times 10^{30}$ kg
Counter Clock Wise Attractive
Energy Value of our sun.

New Theories with Interpretations

The attractive value for the sun and the attractive values of the planets take place during the time distance of 247.69 earth years (Pluto's orbit distance in earth years)

These are all Attractive Values as they are COUNTER CLOCKWISE ROTATIONS.

With respect to our galaxy's clockwise rotation.

CHAPTER 17   PART 3

REPULSION ENERGY VALUE OF THE SUN

There must be many types of galactic energy in our galaxy space. Please read my article "Energy and Our Galactic and Extra Galactic Energy." Chapter 16

When a Mass (MWE) moves through this galactic space energy an energy is produced in the MWE that is an attraction or repulsion energy.

All MWE moving in the same direction in the same galactic energy will have an attractive energy produced in them and will attract each other.

If two MWE are moving in the same galactic energy in opposite directions, the MWE's will have opposing energies and will repel each other.

The sun rotates on its axis once every 36 earth days, counter clockwise.

Physics — Astronomy — Sciences
New Theories with Interpretations

Sun orbital velocity in our galaxy is 220 km/second

220 km/second x 60 = 13,200 km/minute
13,200 km/minute x 60 = 792,000 km/hour
792,000 km/hour x 24 = 19,008,000 km/day
19,008,000 km/day x 365 = 6,937,920,000 km/year

Sun orbital velocity in our galaxy is 6,937,920,000 km/earth year.

19,008,000 **x** 365 = 6,937,920 **x** 10^3 km/year sun orbital
km/day   earth   velocity in our galaxy
Sun orbital days/year
velocity

6,937,920 **x** 10^3 km/year **x** 247.69 years
sun orbital distance   Pluto's orbit
for 1 year   in years.

▶ = 1,718,453,405 **x** 10^3 km/247.69 years
sun orbit distance for 247.69 years

1,718,453,405 **x** 10^3 km/247.69 years
x 1.98 **x** 10^{30} kg sun Mass (MWE)

▶ = 3,402,537,742,000 **x** 10^{30} kg/km/247.69 years
sun repulsion energy
or
3,402,537,742 **x** 10^3 **x** 10^{30} kg/km/247.69 years

3,402,537,742,000 **x** 10^{30} kg/km/247.69 years

Sun Repulsion Energy

-4,973 **x** 10^{30} kg/km/247.69 years

Sun Attraction Energy

3,402,537,737,027 **x** 10^{30} kg/km 247.69
years Difference in Favor Sun Repulsion Energy

All this could be done other ways or by some division could be put on a one earth year basis.

So, I will put the sun repulsion, sun attraction and difference on a one earth year basis.

$$\frac{3,402,537,742,000 \textbf{ x } 10^{30} \text{ kg/km}}{247.69 \text{ years}}$$

=13,737,081,600 **x** 10^{30} kg/km
sun repulsion energy for 1 earth year

$\frac{4,973 \textbf{ x } 10^{30} \text{ kg/km}}{247.69 \text{ years}}$ = 20.08 **x** 10^{30} kg/km sun attraction energy
for 1 earth year

13,737,081,600.00 **x** 10^{30} sun repulsion energy

-20.08 **x** 10^{30} sun attraction energy

13,737,081.579.92 **x** 10^{30} difference, repulsion in favor for sun

All 3 figures above are for 1 earth year.

99

Physics — Astronomy — Sciences
New Theories with Interpretations

CHAPTER 17   PART 4

THE DEATH OF MODERN GRAVITY THEORY *!*

Now What! The numbers do not support modern gravity theory.

Now all of a sudden our sun has much more repulsion energy than attraction energy.

I and everyone else thought the sun was the big attractor, meaning that the sun, would eventually attract its planets and other surrounding objects into itself.

After doing this research work and coming up with these figures, I have changed by thinking on the subject.

Now, the sun with its overwhelming repulsion energy must be pushing the planets and surrounding objects away from itself, not attracting as we all thought.

Modern theories on gravity are doomed. They are headed for the grave yard. In my way of thinking, modern day gravity is already in the grave yard, dead and buried.

According to modern day gravity theory, the sun has a lot of attraction for the planets and the planets also have attraction for the sun. So why is it that they all are not part of the sun? Why is it that this mutual attraction has not attracted all the planets into the sun?

Why is it that most comets avoid going directly into the sun? All this attraction should bring comets into the sun.

Plus other reasons given throughout this book.

Please read chapter 4, "Galactic Space Medium Centrifugal Energy."

CHAPTER 17 PART 5

MOVEMENT OF OUR SOLAR SYSTEM IN OUR GALAXY

Actually the planets do not move in a true ellipse as they move in their orbit about the sun, as is drawn on a piece of flat paper.

The reason for this is — while the planets are moving in their counter clockwise ellipse orbit about the sun — they are also; at the same time moving in our galaxy in a clockwise movement. So, this would indicate an elliptic screw type of movement for each of the planets. Please refer to drawing (17-5) 1.

What is the time-distance for "X"?

We know that our sun rotates clockwise around the center of our galaxy. This takes approximately 200 million earth years (200×10^6).

The time-distance for "X", which is from the starting point of "X" on an ellipse to the starting point of the following ellipse. This is equal to one earth year.

Clockwise movement of our solar system in our galaxy

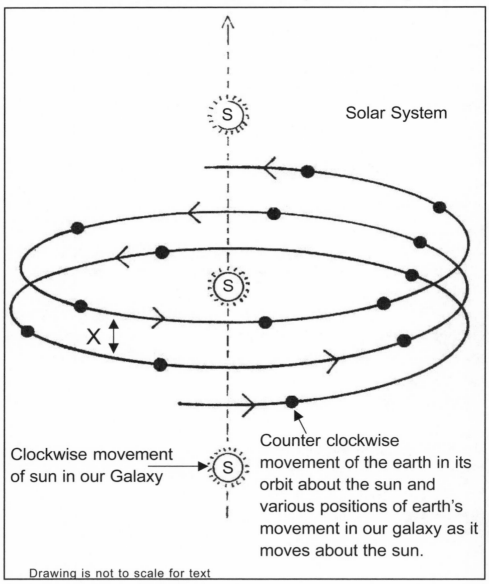

Solar System

X

Clockwise movement
of sun in our Galaxy

Counter clockwise
movement of the earth in its
orbit about the sun and
various positions of earth's
movement in our galaxy as it
moves about the sun.

Drawing is not to scale for text

Drawing (17-5) 1

From the above information we can see that the earth makes 200×10^6 elliptic orbits, equal to 200×10^6 earth years, in one rotation about the center of our galaxy. So; this would indicate that the time-distance "X" is equal to the circumference of the earth's elliptic orbit around our sun. See drawing (17-5) 1. Drawing not to scale for text.

What is the orientation of the earths's ecliptic plane as it rotates with the sun in its orbit in our galaxy?

Remember we have two movements.
1. The earth rotates counter clockwise in its elliptic orbit about our sun.

2. The sun rotates clockwise in its orbit about the center of our galaxy.

These two movements going on a the same time will produce the elliptic screw type of movement.

What is the time-distance of "X"?

At the present time I don not know, and do not have the time to work on the answer.

Maybe some of you readers can work up the answer.

Physics — Astronomy — Sciences
New Theories with Interpretations

CHAPTER 18

OUR SUN, REPULSION ENERGY AND ATTRACTION ENERGY

For the earth we have a very good record of evidence of facts as to what happened in its past.

The facts are in geologic evidence we have here on earth.

There is so much for the record. Fossils of all kinds: shells, fish, dinosaurs, all types of reptiles and hundreds of other fossils.

Then there is all this stored energy: coal, oil, gas and other forms of stored energy.

One could go on and on about this past recorded record of evidence here on earth.

If one looks at this past record, they will see that in the past there were times when energy from the sun was much more in abundance than it is now.

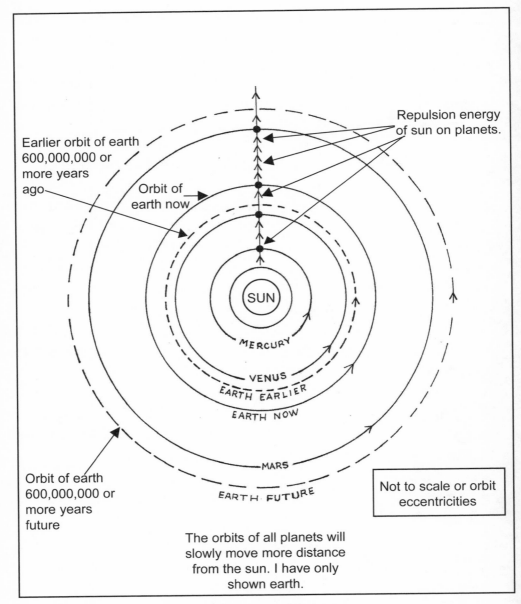

Repulsion energy of sun on planets.

Earlier orbit of earth 600,000,000 or more years ago

Orbit of earth now

Orbit of earth 600,000,000 or more years future

Not to scale or orbit eccentricities

SUN

MERCURY

VENUS

EARTH EARLIER

EARTH NOW

MARS

EARTH FUTURE

The orbits of all planets will slowly move more distance from the sun. I have only shown earth.

Drawing 18-1

According to my theory on Repulsion Energy from the sun, places the planets much closer to the sun than they are now.

The Repulsion Energy of the sun has moved the orbits of the planets further and further from the sun as distance-time move on, or really as our solar system moves in our galaxy.

Please refer to drawing (18-1) for more detail information.

The earth, and other planets, must have been closer to the sun billions of years ago. At that time, they must have had a faster orbital period and a faster axis rotation, even the axis of inclination (23-1/2 degrees from vertical to plane of earth's orbit) may have been different.

Plenty of sunshine, heat, rain, lighting (to produce nitrogen fertilizer). All vegetative matter grew very rampant, large animals were in abundance as were many other forms of life.

Some Dinosaurs were 65 feet (19.8 meters) to 85 feet (25.9 meters) long and weighing as much as 10 short tons (9.07 metric tons) or more.

Just think of how much food large animals of this size require each day.

This was earth's "Golden Era".

As the repulsion energy from the sun caused the orbits to slowly move to larger orbits, all this "Golden Era" for the earth is in the past. Could this have been the cause of the Dinosaur extinction?

New Theories with Interpretations

If one compares the earth of today with the earth of its "Golden Era," one can see that its future does not look too good.

In the future, billions of years from now, the oceans will be frozen and all life will be extinct. The earth will just be another lump of matter in a more distance orbit about the sun.

From earth fossils, we have a record to show that the earth today is almost a desert compared to the earth of the "GOLDEN ERA."

CHAPTER 19

VOLKMANN THEORY ON PLANET FORMATION
A NEW THEORY

Now we have seen that our sun has a lot more repulsion energy than attraction energy, brings a new thought on the formation of the planets, comets and all the other material moving about our sun.

At the time of planet formation, our sun's energy doiman must have been much larger than it is now. Its energy domain was probably out as far as the planet Pluto in now or farther.

At that time, our sun was a rotating ball of energy and it was creating more energy with-in itself.

What happens when this ball of energy keeps producing energy with-in itself. It could explode if there are energy receivers out there, but there were no energy receivers out there to receive any of this tremendous excess energy. What other choice does the energy have? It has only one choice, that is to convert to Mass With Energy. So, here we have energy being converted to MWE.

This process brought about formation of the planets, comets and other material moving about the sun.

Please read chapter 20 "Formation Energy."

CHAPTER 20

FORMATION ENERGY—THE BEGINING

At this point it is time to introduce a new type of energy. Different from the Mass With Energy type and the Electromagnetic Spectrum type.

The Mass With Energy type is what we usually associate with the movements of MWE from one of its energy levels to another energy level.

The Electromagnetic Spectrum Energy type involves Electromagnetic Spectrum Energy movements.

This new type of energy I call FORMATION ENERGY, because it is the type of energy that was used to form our Mass With Energy and the Electromagnetic Spectrum Energy at the forming time of our solar system.

What is this FORMATION ENERGY? It is something that we know very little about, in fact almost nothing, because we live in an environment of Mass With Energy. So, this FORMATION ENERGY is really out of our knowledge realm. All we can do at the present time is to speculate on its nature.

My thinking is this FORMATION ENERGY is something not present here on earth, but we may see and detect its presence in the outer universe. For example: suppose we are looking at the night sky and then, all of a sudden in a blank spot a light appears, behold a new star! Maybe! What happened? Here we saw FORMATION ENERGY being transformed into Electromagnetic Energy. After all what we see is light and light is Electromagnetic Energy. We could also be receiving Radio Energy or other forms of Electromagnetic Spectrum Energy not detected by our eyes, but detected by our Radio Energy receivers or other Electromagnetic Spectrum detectors.

Now, what about MWE being formed by the FORMATION ENERGY? This can also happen. MWE and EMSE, both maybe formed at the same time, or just Mass With Energy alone.

If MWE were formed alone, the chances of detecting it would be remote as it would be dark and not radiate energy. If it reflected energy—as our moon—we could detect it. Also, if a detecable energy source moved in back of the MWE or if the MWE moved in front of a detecable energy source, then it would be detectable.

Another event could take place, for example: suppose the FORMATION ENERGY transformed into all Electromagnetic Spectrum Energy, it could go to many forms of EMS Energy— light, radio, x-ray, etc., or to a mixture of EMS Energy.

114

Let us look at one form of detectable EMS Energy from outer space. Radio Energy, we can detect the Radio Energy with our radio receivers and spot the area of its origin. In most of these areas, there is no detectable MWE. This tells us that the FORMATION ENERGY from these areas has been transformed to all Electromagnetic Spectrum Energy.

When all the EMS Energy has gone to receivers of the energy, then there is an area of no FORMATION ENERGY.

SUMMARY:

There are 3 ways the FORMATION ENERGY can go.

1. To all MWE.   FE $\longrightarrow$ MWE

2. To all Electromagnetic Spectrum Energy. FE $\longrightarrow$ EMSE

3. To a mix of MWE and Electromagnetic Spectrum Energy. FE $\longrightarrow$ MWE + EMSE

Physics — Astronomy — Sciences
New Theories with Interpretations

SOME NEW CONCEPTS I HAVE PRESENTED IN THIS BOOK

1. A new view to what is now called Mass. The atom is made into two parts, the nucleus being Mass and outside the nucleus we have spheres of energy. Chapter 1 and 2

2. When all Mass has been converted to energy, then there is no mass just energy. Chapter 1 and 2

3. Galactic Space Medium Energy. Many forms of energy exist in the galactic space. Chapter 3

4. Galactic Space Medium Centrifugal Energy. This is energy introduced into a MWE by its rotation in the GSME. Chapter 4

5. Resonance acceptance. This is a common effect. A sender can not send energy unless there is a receiver to receive that energy. Chapters 5 and 6

6. Volkmann Effect. This is the back-flux energy produced by a moving MWE. It is a self produced movement resistance. Chapter 7

7. Contraction of length by a moving MWE. There is no contraction of length of a moving MWE. It is a contraction of its moving distance due to medium energy loss and the Volkmann Effect. Chapter 8

8. Contraction of circumference of a rotating MWE. This is a contraction of the circumference of a moving MWE, due to loss of energy of the MWE, from the medium the MWE is rotating in and the Volkmann Effect. Chapter 9

9. Clockwise rotation of an elliptical spiral. Chapter 9
   Counter Clockwise rotation of an elliptical spiral. Chapter 9

10. There can be expansion of a moving MWE circumference. Chapter 9

11. Electromagnetic spectrum consists of pulses of different lengths. Each pulse length has the same energy value. A short pulse has the same energy value as a long pulse. Each pulse length has the same speed. You may ask how can each pulse length have the same speed, and yet have the same energy value for any pulse length.

If a pulse length is A to B and another pulse length is 3 times A to B, and yet both have the same energy value, how can this be? Let's assume pulse length A to B has X energy value, should not pulse length 3 times A to B be equal to 3X energy value? No.

The reason a pulse length A to B and a pulse length 3 times A to B have the same speed and the same energy valve is because they are electromagnetic spectrum pulses and do not have a back-flux energy loss. Chapter 10-2

One thing that needs to be clarified is that speed and distance are not the same. For example A to B is one distance and 3 times A to B is 3 distances. Let us assume the speed A to B is 1 meter per second, therefore, 3 times A to B would be 3 meters in 3 seconds. So we have one pulse length at 1 meter length in one second and we have another pulse length at 3 meters length in 3 seconds. Each pulse was moving at the same speed of 1 meter per second. Chapter 10-2

12. Pulse length "as a unit" (AAU) speed is different from pulse length speed explained above. A pulse length can be A to B or 3 times A to B or 10 times A to B. The speed of the pulse length "as a unit," (AAU) is the same for all pulse lengths in a vacuum Chapter 10-3

13. Electromagnetic spectrum energy from vast distances can move vast distances because electromagnetic spectrum pulses produce no back-flux resistance energy, Volkmann Effect, to slow them down. Chapter 10-4

14. Electromagnetic spectrum pulse speed "as a unit" (AAU) in a transparent Mass With Energy medium. This is where the speed

117

of the EMS pulse speed AAU changes speed due to the back-flux energy caused by the MWE medium in which the pulse is moving. Chapter 10-5

15. There are three speeds in my new electromagnetic spectrum pulse theory: Chapter 10-6
A) speed time of a pulse length
B) speed time of a pulse length As A Unit (AAU) in a vacuum
C) pulse length speed time AAU in a transparent MWE medium

16. Flow of electricity—flow of electrons or flow of magnetism? There is the possibility there may be two types of electricity, the electron flow type and the magnetic flow type. Chapter 11

17. Will an object (a Mass With Energy) launched into space ever stop? Yes, due to the Volkmann Effect, back-flux resistance energy. There are two resistances to this movement. Chapter 12
A) energy value loss is a resistance
B) back-flux energy is a resistance.

18. Energy value loss is a resistance. The loss of energy value from a moving MWE means that the remaining energy value has to move the same amount of MWE with less energy. Chapter12

19. Distance and time are the same when a Mass With Energy and movement of this MWE are involved. Chapter 15

20. Galactic energy and extra galactic energy—there are many types of galactic and extra galactic energy. Some we know. There are more that we do not know. Chapter 16

21. The lowest energy level that is possible is when there is no Mass With Energy left for energy to move in to or out of. At this state all the Mass With Energy has been converted to electromagnetic energy and there is no Mass With Energy left. Chapter16

22. Mass With Energy movements in the same directions attract each

other. Chapter 17-1

23. Mass With Energy movements in opposite directions repel each other. Chapter17-1

24. The sun has more repulsion energy than attraction energy. Chapters 17-3 and 18

25. The sun and all nine planets have less attraction energy than the sun's repulsion energy. Chapter 17-2

26. In the future billions of years from now, the oceans will be frozen and all life will be extinct. Earth will just be another lump of matter in a more distance orbit about the sun. Chapter 18

27. Volkmann Theory on Planet Formation—A New Theory. Formation of planets by the process of transformation of energy to Mass With Energy. Chapter 19

28. Our sun at formation time was a much larger sphere of energy. At this time it was still producing energy within itself. This excess energy had no place to go, as there were no receivers for this excess energy, so this excess energy went from energy to Mass With Energy. These new formed MWE objects are the planets and other objects in orbit about the sun. Here we see the transformation of energy to Mass With Energy. Chapter 18

29. The planets, billions of years ago the planets were much closer to the sun than they are now. The earth was in its "Golden Era". Lots of sunshine, plenty of warmth, plants grew in abundance, many large animals, etc. This was earth's "Golden Era".Today earth is like a desert compared to earth's "Golden Era". All this orbit change due to the sun's repulsion energy, earth's "Golden Era" is gone. Chapter 18

30. Movement of our solar system in our Galaxy. Chapter 17-5

INDEX